POP SMOKE & PRAY

Pop Smoke & Pray or *Laughing 'til the Barrel Melts*
Copyright © 2008 by Frank Barry Smith
All Rights Reserved

ISBN: 978-0-6151-7180-7

:: TRANSMISSION BOOKS ::
san francisco.ca

POP SMOKE & PRAY
or
LAUGHING 'TIL THE BARREL MELTS

Frank Barry Smith

TRANSMISSION BOOKS
2008

CONTENTS

To Bob and Pat Stallman, the Idaho Kids   11
Field Day   14
Dry Monsoon   16
Another Day   17
Poem at War   19
Three Poems for My Sister   20
Tiger   23
Just Beyond Winter   26
Mizutami, Poem One   28
Mizutami, Poem Two   29
Angel   30
Willie   34
Days for Guy   36
David, The Crispy King of Crazyweed   43
Fire Base Barbara   45
Willie   46
Aaron Rosenstreich   47
To the Infantry   48
Ecclesiastes   49
Prayer   50
Revolution   51
The Middle   52

POP SMOKE & PRAY
or
LAUGHING 'TIL THE BARREL MELTS

TO BOB AND PAT STALLMAN
the Idaho Kids

I had promised to write long letters
but it was Summer
and I had sat by the Bay
hating my job and saying nothing.
I didn't write anything down,
even in the shower
where no one heard.
I drank July off the wall

In August I imagined you
plummeting like a young bird
toward the smoking forests of Montana;
waiting for the round pop
of the parachute
while Pat shelved soup cans
singing to the record player
uncertain about dinner.

I boarded long-distance busses
and rode drunk
across the surface of California
until I found myself in Sacramento
in September
and fled to Oregon
becoming
a part-time school teacher.

I dried in the Klamath wind.

By then you'd returned to
The City
to find another apartment.
I watched the snow fall
among red drying apples
that still hung from the leafless trees
beyond my land-locked window.

You moved from lectures
when I was lecturing
the faces of the children
of Modoc and Klamath.
We had our places

in rooms in America.
And then it was Christmas
and I received a green card
saying: "We are alive,
and in a hurry,
and there is always
love here."
I noticed that we had
the same address
in different towns.

In February, after packing,
I drove South
through a break in the weather.
The Government was writing me
from an office in California.
I went to have myself inspected
in Fresno,
thinking they could not
know of the war there
and I wouldn't be called.

It didn't work.

When I saw you again,
you said, "I'll get beer
Pat will be home soon,
and pregnant."
And she was.
We found ourselves laughing
all the way through April
when we pushed through
rush hour traffic
with your bed in the back
of my truck to lay a quick claim
on your new house.
Later, leaving that house
I met your mailman
who thought I was you.
He gave me the white
government envelope
and I took it upstairs
into Pat's anger.

This morning my own mail
was the same
printed in small letters:
"approval not required"

I had promised to write
long letters,
but the Summer is coming on.

MARCH 1968

FIELD DAY

                How can you splint
                the homesick fear
                of a foreign death
                or tourniquet
                the long-ago
                Texas Christmas
                day-dreams
                pouring from the mouth
                of a red-headed sergeant
                called Albie?

New fatigues bloused
into shiny black
and nylon boots
swung
in the helicopter air
above the cratered
jungle mountains
named Rocket Ridge.

"I've never seen a war before,"
I'd said to Pat.
"there are poems there, waiting."

But now,
eagle screaming scared
shitless in the streaming air
I could not find
poetry here,
and hid behind the medicine mask:
"Pain is a symptom
of disease or injury;
Psychic pain manifests itself..."
This catechism of my training
canted the numbing prayers,
while between my knees and boots
the sky slid above to behind
and faced me to the defoliate
brown-gray stain
in the wide green
where a yellow blossom of smoke
marked the hub of my future

spiraling me at eighty knots
into the smiles and stares
with:
"Thank God you're here"
and the curse:
"Hey you cherry.
Where's you're rifle?
You better best not expect
t'get one here.
This'll cost you ...
And another voice said
"Don't mean nothing, Ridge,
's the Doc."
And Ridge's face opened
into a smile and
 "Hey, help you with the gear?
You got Tiger Tonight."
            Shit.
And he shrugged, smiling,
"Sorry— first night in bush
but ambush squad needs a doc.
Name's Ridgerunner,
Platoon leader here
until we get a lou."
And coffee was made
and we sat talking like friends
gone camping
of news from home,
hamburgers,
french fries,
and absent loves,
bringing
each longing
like gifts to a feast—
and my six-month fight
with the airborne-loving
rifle-humping infantry
stopped.

DRY MONSOON

When the blades stopped turning
and the turbines spun to silence
the word came down the weather
and the weather came down
from the black hot sky
and sifted the ground
through slits
in the wind-bowed tent walls
where we waited
listening to A.F.V.N.
on the portable radio
without light or air power
while the anchored choppers rocked
and the war stopped
for the moving air.

ANOTHER DAY

Riffing that ridge line
in those hot woods
almost half that day,
angered by heavy packs,
wait-a-minute vines
that caught jackets,
straps, helmet covers,
skin,
and that constant order
to keep moving,
I saw the future then—
the short-sighted near-future
across that next tree-bare
ridge break,
Rolling Thundered deep dust thick,
There, on that next ridge top
behind that forest foliaged wall,
 was someone's death place
in fight time.
Gun fight time.
I did not tell.
How can you say
"I have seen the future,
pass it on?"

A small wound
could take me home,
and I wished for one.
A small one. Painless,
on some yet unknown part
of me
I would not miss.
Fine dust covered my boot tops
then and now
deep in that ridge split.
One more ridge to climb.
Choose one:
Leg. Shoulder. Hip.
Abdomen?
No.
Not there.
The climb kept up the sweat.

But it came too fast
flashing
into gun smell,
stripping bullet sounds
in my own air.
Rifles snapping, rolling
in swimming time
yanking the drop-snap
on my ruck
spinning shoulders free
fingers grabbing straps
on the aid kit flying
into the blankets of air
to shield me
as I fell flat to the warm ground
chuckling into the singing air
and I ran
up the bare ridge
through the green wall
to a death
that was not mine,
laughing.

POEM AT WAR
For Thomas St.Onge

After we made the landing zone
I found Norm, who said
you'd disappeared in flash blast
before you'd known.

Later,
meeting across a shattered arm
that was neither his nor mine,
Tunney asked:
"You a medic?"
And we argued:
Dextran or albumin.
Looking for an 18 gauge vein
until the sounds of flying metal
brought us flat to the ground
to lie among those parts
that had once turned to me
laughing
from your radio handset
that your bunker was washing
down the hill
in the waterfall rain
with your platoon sergeant inside.

But looking at you then
in that flesh burnt air
and fly-buzz
of the sudden quiet
I couldn't think of you, Tom.
I was only glad
your scattered flesh
was not my own.

THREE POEMS FOR MY SISTER

I. HOME SONG

It's late evening
and this mountain
where I've come to live
between my liquid fears
and fantasy patrols
shadows this northern valley
and the war.
Looking in the cracked mirror
I find my face is etched with dust,
and I watch those black lines
frame my laughter
for I am at home again with myself
as I take up your letter
and read each rain-splashed line:

That wish for peace, at last
and those not-words at all
but music drawn upon the page.

Looking North, Tonkin Gulf is dark
and below Rocket Ridge
the cavalry clanks in circles
on the battle plain
while Snake, on the slope
is smoking dope and singing.
Knapp takes his guitar,
I my harmonica
and Snake sings us home.

II VISION FOR THE YEARS

Smile your Rembrandt smile.
Dance your lunar dance.
I take your wishes with me
to help my Friendly stance.

Turn your face into the wind
and let your hair go free
this world's too full of images
you shouldn't want to see.

"All things that live are Holy"
"Praise to the end" and more;
my saints have taught me wholly
to reach within this war.

And reaching in I turn a wish
a blessing oil upon your head
to see you with your daughters
as they dance upon the sand:
An apple heart within ones hand
the other, light with song
While you curl your toes
into the ground
remembering the sound
remembering the music
the music of the moon.

III HELICOPTER DAYS,
        AMPHETAMINE NIGHTS

Three-quarter ton trucks
blistered feet and heavy tanks.
I'm given this day
my daily bread
insanity of peasants
in the night
and two packs of Winstons
to make the world safe
for someone else.

I am lost
to the politics of Paris
jungle trails, hemostats
primary closures and tourniquets.

I breath among pain
and drink my sleep
to hold memory
above my sweat.

TIGER

Carl's Cajun accent announced
"There's a tiger in the mess tent."

And he shut the aid station door
behind him
and because codes
had become conversation,
I thought the ambush squad
was drinking coffee
before moving out,
and I turned to hide in sleep
until Carl's chambering rifle clatter
burned the sleep from my belly
and my eyes opened to the listening air
and into the shimmering night
that blew
between the wet metal panels
of the unbagged wall where I lay
while the sounds
of the changing earth
broke on my ears
into grass touching in the wind
stones kicked,
a cough
from a bunker,
rifles slap-jacking loads
and the metal tracks that clanked
on the distant armored plain, below.

So I breathe with the mountain wind
crippled with the two-legged sense:
blind to the dark
and near deaf to the living night.

How may lives had been spent
wolfing the tiger
or tigering the wolf
dark in the oaken forests
or tall on the blowing steppes
to bring me to this Asian mountain
to feel this again?

We   crouch at the door,
cough far into the liquid night
and pound in the blood
with and without that fear of death
that is mine and ours.
I gather wound packs, cravats
and instruments
pitying that tiger
his lonely singularity.
We spread our hands
on these mountains
and our voice streams silent
through the radio air.
We make night flare into day
splash jellied fire from the sky,
bring on the flying rifles of the sun
and see yellow day in the starlit dark.

This tiger's life
moves with his lone choice
and single hunger—
And that belly drive
that brought him here
is known
 and given space.
For we have hunted hungry
in that high wood.

Eat tiger, we have more food now
than we want to carry,
and we are going
deep in the dark
as soon as the sun.

Eat tiger,
we stripped your forest
and burned your food
as big as elephants—
but not for you.
Choke out your hunger
in the chocolate bars,
turkey loaves and ice cream,
and go quiet into this hot night
to sleep your tiger sleep
in the steaming leaves.

Tiger widens on the nostrils
and is gone
and Carl, unchambering
moves from the door.
"All weapons will be disarmed
on these premises except..."
and I am lost again in the infantry
in a country that is not mine
on a khaki sleeping bag
with my equipment
and fear.

JUST BEYOND WINTER

                Awakened at 4 AM for reveille
                the 5th of June 1968
                the radio morning news broke on my ears
                to hurt my heart too much for tears.

Only He knew that deal
repeated in the silence
of this prayer:

Ten more years
for you
in trade
for mine.

He knew a bad risk.

Less than six months later
He showed me:

Face shoved flat to that ant-run earth
raging silent prayers for life and home
and when the air burning all
of the jellied gas
fell from friendly fire misjudgment
toward me and Southeast Asia:
Brown's face cut into memory
like crystal terror
shouting
GET DOWN GET DOWN GET DOWN

the flesh prefers life
and I understood St. Peter
before the crow.

All that June Texas day
I watched the garrison flag
as if by faith, it would not fly
below full staff.

I called that afternoon to California
and told them,
as if I could control
anything
that you would be all right.

Then
you got away
Bobby.

I remembered you'd turned
before climbing up
on that car trunk
in that blowing
San Francisco University night,
saying
"No, there will never
be enough time."

And you rode off forever,
with those two sisters
in billowing habits
one to either side
laughing and waving
like a football hero
after victory.

I couldn't write this down
until now
but that decade of the deal
I failed to make
will be ending soon:
over there,
just beyond Winter.

MIZUTAMI

Poem One

Flying out of dirt, despair and death
your fresh light
does not mirror on my face too well.
Guarded like a camp at war
I don't respond when probed,
waiting to see your full strength.
I do not bow, or show my thanks.

Forgive me, please
and let this foreign English
thank you.
For you lead me
out of war
to peace
and did not stop to ask:
"Is this the way?"

MIZUTAMI

Poem Two

Images of friend burning,
intestinal flesh scattered on leaves
gives way to you
and I am escaped
for these few minutes
of beer and laughter.

TOKYO
August 16, 1969

ANGEL

                  for Rodriguez
                  who always knew
                  who he was

In the jungle quiet
of the green evening
we settled to ambush,
beside that trail
tired, scratching,
 grumbling and laughing.

Captain is a killing man.

I'd rather be in Philadelphia.

I spread my gear around me
like a wall.
        I remember Jay
went in a flash from sleep
to death.
Was that last night, or the night before:

No.

It took us three days
              or four
to send his body back.
His boots sticking out
under his pancho liner
forever.

Trip flares set.
Claymores planted and plugged.
But the word
kept passing:

Second.

Second's not set.

Still moving.
Something's wrong.

Dark came and shrank the faith;
no cooking, no smoking, no moving, no joking.

Captain wants a killing.

What a way to earn a living.

Radio whisper, broken squelch.

Mongoose chatter
from the trees
means sleep without snake
tonight.
God bless you
Riki-Tiki-Tavi.

Angel's got a laughing gun:
Angels' got no helmet
Threw it away,
got busted.
Lt.'s got a worried face
can't find second
can't take chances
can't figure.

MOVEMENT.
Movement.
Movement on the trail.

Pray for monkeys, pray for peace,
pray for
POP
goes the weasel flash blinding
glare in the black night
scuffle on the trail
voices shout
and claymore rip blasts flash
Rends time and the jungle
screaming

OH GOD DAMN
GOD DAMN
I'M HIT.

English.

Lt. shouts for gunners
fear confused to his eyes

are they ours?
Are they Second?

Grab kit and run
to the trail
flared brighter than day
shadows moving
swaying from the parachute lights
darker than sight.
Angel's on my shoulder yelling
"cover the doc
"cover the doc
"we smoked Second!"
Angel's my guardian
machine gun crazy man.
Lt. checks fire.
Second's leader's off the trail
blown off
butt full of frags
screaming gibberish pain.

CALL DUST OFF
pass it back
pass it back to com.

Captain's got the red ass.

Dust-off lights the sky
Fourth of July in the Jungle
gun ships slap and rap
in the gun run air
and rip the woods
for Dusty.

Angel's got a laughing face
Captain's got the ass
Lt.'s got a crying man
trigger unhappy claymore man
says "Not your fault.
"Not your fault.
"You done good."
I've got basket patients
swinging skyward screaming pain
and others riding penetrators
laughing
getting over easy.

Captain's here.

—Got a helmet left for the Gunner?—
"No sir,
"sent 'em off with Dusty".
Angel's got a laughing face

WILLIE

                        You see Lord,
                        we took care
                        of one another
                        on that long road
                        to glory.

On that Texas Sergeant's street
you were kidded for you bulk,
your Baby Huey look and lisp
but you were faithful to the Jew
and smiled when you turned
your massive cheek.

Later when you came to the war
where I was
You still wouldn't drink
with Jones and me
so we found you a daytime soda
in the bottom ice of the Mermite Can
and talked of suturing
splinting, morphine and Texas,
and mostly worry
that we would not know enough
when the time came.

After our first assault
in the A Shau
when your company
passed through mine
on that ridge position in the rain
I found you'd changed.
Those months had made you
muscled and certain.
But your gentleness remained.
You followed the carpenter
as best you could.
You wouldn't take a rifle
on that second hard jump
in the A Shau—
and it was the hill this time:
Dong Ap Bia,

and Nick and Petrie and Bob
all told you
not to go up again,
but you were Doc Kirkland,
a target big as the sun
and your people were calling to you for help.
So you made the news back home
with Nick and Sovetsky
trying to breath life
back into you
after you'd lain
on that hill
too long.

May 1969
Camp Evans
RVN

DAYS FOR GUY

      Joseph Guy LaPointe
      Conscientious Objector
      and Combat Medic
      was killed in action
      2 June 1969
      in the Republic of Viet Nam

MAY 1969, Fort Sam Houston, Texas

    You held hands with Kansas City
    for too long,
    and the Cumberland in Summer
    breathed though your lungs
    to make Ohio your skin—
    so much that
    when the government papers came,
    confining you to Texas and the Army
    your eyes wanted Dayton too much
    to cry.

    Still you sang.

    You said Canada
    was foreign to you,
    and Nova Scotia ran Autumn
    in your veins.
    You wouldn't turn
    North to Freedom.

27 AUGUST 1968, Three-day Pass

    Leaving San Antonio
    we rode north to Dallas,
    and on that road, drinking wine,
    you named the birds,
    the plants, the small animals
    for me— I listened
    as you read the land,
    and when you sang,
    it was the same:
    your gentle love
    sang though your voice and hands.

    Later, when you called
    all the way from Dallas
    to your pregnant wife
    your eyes were gone to Dayton
    in Ohio, watching her grow.

    You were too innocent
    for honesty.

4 NOVEMBER 1968,   Oakland Army Depot

    Beyond the green warehouse
    the politician's words that kill
    and flag that files an unkept promise
    brushed on your skin.
    The touch was lost.
    America was not theirs
    it was not there.
    We followed the taped red line
    and left our baggage in the dark.

NOVEMBER 1968, San Francisco AWOL

    In that stolen time
    we stood on Ocean Beach
    while you taught me
    other songs to sing,
    saying you wouldn't mind
    the coming year—
    next Fall would be here soon.

    I didn't want to take you
    from that place where you stood
    throwing stones at the sky,
    but words were raging
    form the capitals of the world
    and the killing time was coming.

12 NOVEMBER 1968, Bien Hoa, RVN

    Leaning on the sandbags
    encasing the wooden
    and wire-screened hooch
    beside the bomber's locking radar station
    we read each other's orders,
    smoking.
    They were all words and numbers then,
    and we spoke only of memories.
    I copied your address
    and lost it.

2 JUNE 1969, Hue, RVN

    I watched the wide river
    from my bunker top
    while the pric 25
    stoned my radio ears
    telling me in static rasps
    that a dying time was near—
    I thought it was my own.

    Tomorrow
    we would relieve
    the Second
    of the Seventeenth Cavalry.

    It was all words
    and numbers.

OCTOBER 1969, America

    In Kansas, the wheat and corn
    have been harvested, shipped and sold,
    the wild geese are escaped South
    and soon the snows will cover
    the Dakotas and Wyoming.
    I want to hear you
    sing this Winter coming on.

    The sun burns southward.
    Voices stall through the capitals
    and fade in the air—

    But in America
    who is left to name
    those small animals
    moving through the snow,
    or tell the histories
    of each brittle weed
    standing frozen in the wind?

October 5, 1969
Phong Dien, RVN

DAVID
The Cripsy King Of Crazyweed

The surgeon didn't like his eyes
and sent him to the field again,
so he went back to his people
on village security
until the surgeon thought
and the sergeant thought
David had enough
and they called him back.
But he wouldn't come
for two months.
And when he finally came
the surgeon didn't like those eyes
that swam between poppy smoke
and crazyweed
trying not to see
when his wife wrote insanity
in suicide letters
addressed 'David Sr.'
sending pictures of the kids
smearing lipstick on the envelopes
and tears along the words
until his hands shook
as he placed the equipment
for the surgeon.

And so the surgeon thought
and the first sergeant thought
and David became
HEAD SHITBURNER
But the degradation
would not fall on him.
In the mornings
he slid out the shortened cans,
poured in the oil and stirred,
saying:

"You've got to get it pasty first."

And he placed all four cans closely,
rolled a wick and birthed his fire.

Flames rose to over fifteen meters,

and they came to watch:
the sergeant, the surgeon
and first pig,
while David stirred and poured oil
and turned,
waving his long stir-stick
flaming with shit and oil
and exclaiming his art
until they fled, shouting orders,
giving him Blakely,
his assistant.
They built a house
where he could burn shit
all day
even if it rained.
A fuel rack was built
"To draw the oil", he'd said.
And a Jeep was given
for trips and needs
and a driver
because the surgeon didn't
trust David's eyes.

Under the heavy sky
Thick with coming rain
all could hear that shout to Blakely:

"Is it cripsy Yet?"

Or in the hot sun
when the sergeant sent him students
he could be seen
stripped to the waist,
students seated in the dust
rapt with fascination,
his odd cigarette
hanging from his lip,
explaining each detail of that craft
as he moved four cans in a circle
stirred in the measured oil
and lit the fire.

And they knew,
 sitting there
looking in his eyes
that he was bent
on burning all the shit
from the world.

FIRE BASE BARBARA

I know where I left my sanity.

There,

Below the DMZ looking into Laos,
Far off where the colors fade,
with some of the people
drunk on ten dollar whisky
some on twelve dollar weed
and some on the mix
and each day I went
on a five click riff
and each night
a five man ambush
and each sun passed the sky
and each moon passed the night
in rain
and sleep was left to those
who stayed behind.
Where do you hold to sanity?
I never did again.
And here I am
years later, turning back,
certain that the trail I'd left
would be there.
But was there ever a trail?

WILLIE

I saw you later
In LIFE Magazine
with that week's dead
standing with a soda
in your hand,
although the soda
wasn't shown.

AARON ROSENSTREICH

Rose, today I am so far
from Southeast Asia
and our war with the war
I didn't expect you
to be here again with me
just by seeing your name on an old list
I'd made
when you'd died too
in the Apache Snowdrifts
and no one had time
to stop for Kaddish.

I'd promised
a poem for your then,
when my breath clogged
as I scribed your name
in that small brown notebook
wrapped in that green tape
and waited for control until
I could speak again and move
back into my own life;
but Rose, I don't know how
to write your poem.
I can only write my own.

The week after you'd died
Supply sent your field jacket
instead of mine.
I kept it
until the Inspector General
found it
and wanted to know
if I'd stolen it.
I think we would have laughed
about that.

TO THE INFANTRY

You had your brass, canvas,
rucksacks, Claymores and fatigues,
I had my body and what I'd called
my soul, before we met.
And we differed
about your use of medicine
and people.
You planned To Conserve
The Fighting Strength
and I learned that you meant it—
and what you meant,
And because I had lived near you
for twenty-three years
and sometimes even loved you
I can forgive the changes
you worked in me
but I don't think
even though
even now
I sometimes
wish to lie with you again,
I can forgive you
the friends
you introduced
and took.

ECCLESIASTES

>   Years later,
>   the sun will rise
>   and set
>   on a dead planet
>   spinning in a dead sky.
>
>   Time doesn't move:
>   It fakes it.

Where do you seek a refuge for your soul?
I looked in The Chronicle,
read the labels on Red Mountain Wine,
and telephoned Hawaii once a week.
I watched the twin re-saw rise
four stories into the Raymond rain,
and finding nothing on my own,
thought there was no thing to find.

>   Some men run
>   on borrowed power,
>   and we who follow,
>   pay their bills.

So why not laugh
down the dark street
with me?
What can it hurt?
Why not stand cross-eyed
on Judgment Day:
After all,
look up to God
sitting there
with his fake nose
and glasses.

>   *14 November 1976*
>   *Sacramento, CA*

PRAYER

God,
I remember being drunk one night
and saying
if you didn't take Willie
with You,
Well,
I just didn't want to go.
I'm sorry
but it still goes.

REVOLUTION

John, I told you
there would be tanks
rolling in the streets,
door to door death,
Vengeance on the High Road.
Well, John,
I was wrong.

THE MIDDLE

The time to move beyond
has come.

Back to the vacant fields
of Fresno
or wherever
it was
I got on this thing.

Nothing changes.
Nothing will.

I have made friends and lost them
in ways more quickly than some
but less than others.
I cannot say that I loved them
more than you.
Only that I loved them.

Frank Barry Smith, now retired and living in Washington state, served as a combat medic in the Vietnam War. He studied poetry under Philip Levine, Robert Mezey, and John Logan.

Other titles from TRANSMISSION PRESS

CHAPBOOKS

Larry Kearney - passion
Brandon Brown - 908 - 1078
Mark Lamoureux - TRACELAND
Sabrina Calle - The Gilles Poem: Winter 2006 Collection
Michael Koshkin - Orgy in the Beef Closet
John Sakkis - The Moveable Ones
Dorothea Lasky - Tourmaline

BOOKS

Logan Ryan Smith - STUPID BIRDS

transmissionpress.blogspot.com
transmissionbooks.blogspot.com

www.ingramcontent.com/pod-product-compliance
Ingram Content Group UK Ltd.
Pitfield, Milton Keynes, MK11 3LW, UK
UKHW041433180426
11947UKWH00007B/422